A Year on the Farm

by Paula Peterson

RoseDog Books
PITTSBURGH, PENNSYLVANIA 15238

Rosedog Books
585 Alpha Drive
Suite 103
Pittsburgh, PA 15238
Visit our website at *www.rosedogbookstore.com*

ISBN, 978-1-6376-4489-8
eISBN: 978-1-6376-4538-3

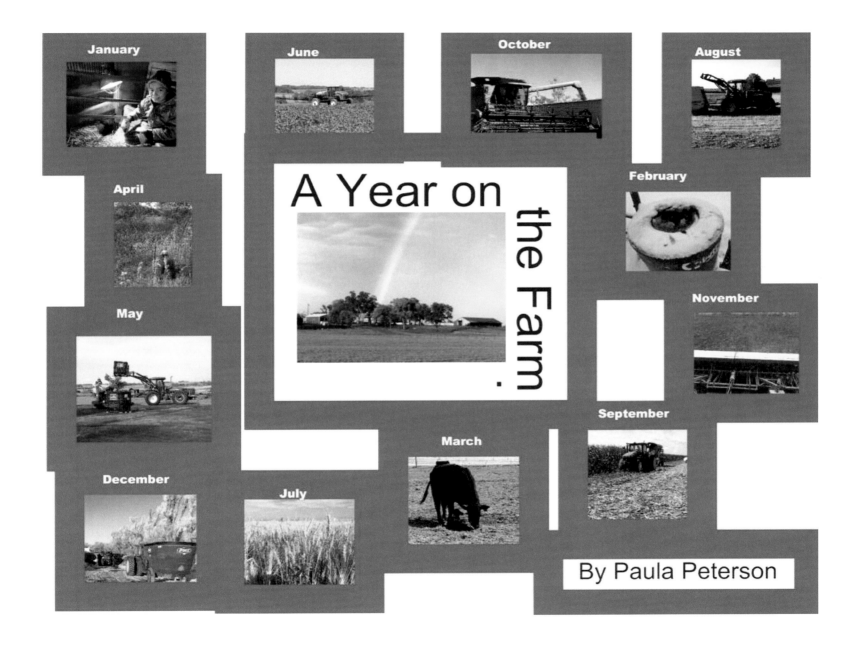

January

June

October

August

A Year on the Farm

February

April

May

November

September

December

July

March

By Paula Peterson

January on this farm will bring you baby lambs.

Did you know sheep have rectangular pupils not round, so they can see almost 300 degrees.

Lambs that are born here get
to visit schools
so children can meet sheep.
They also get to compete at
County fair.

February on this farm means chopping ice so the cows have fresh water to drink.

As a rule of thumb, most cows during cold weather need 1 gallon of water per 100 pounds of body weight. Most mature cows weigh between 1200 and 1400 pounds so that means they need between 12 and 14 gallons of water every day.

March on this farm is the beginning of calving season. Calving season runs from the middle of March to the middle of May.

The average weight of a new calf is between 55 to 75 pounds on this farm.
The calves will stay with their mothers until they are about eight months old.
At eight months old they will weigh between 500 and 600 pounds.

April on this farm is when it is important to get fences checked
on the pastures the cows will be living in for the next five months.

The pastures on this farm have cool season and warm season grasses so the cows have feed all spring and summer.

May on this farm is when corn and soybeans are planted.

For every silk on an ear of corn one kernel can grow.

Ink from soybeans is used in newspapers and textbooks.

June on this farm is when we spray for weeds that take away the nutrients from the soil which hurts the corn and soybeans.

On this farm the pastures are sprayed to prevent weeds from pushing out the grasses the cows need for feed for the summer. Healthy grass makes healthy cows.

July on this farm is when wheat is ready to be harvested. The kernels from the wheat can be used for feed or flour, while the straw will be bedding for the cows when they start to calf in the spring.

Wheat is the most harvested grain in the world. It can be grown on every continent except Antarctica.

August on this farm is when alfalfa is cut and put into bags or bales. This will be the feed for the cattle during the winter.

Alfalfa has the most nutrients of any forage crop. Cows need good feed so they can grow just like people need good food.

September on this farm is when corn is chopped for silage.
Silage is corn that is chopped when it is very green and then packed in a bag or pile.
It is then sealed tight so the corn and stalks can bake into very good feed for cattle.

October on this farm is when we harvest the corn and soybeans that were planted in May.

November on this farm is when wheat gets planted. This farm grows winter wheat so it needs the cold weather of winter to help it grow properly.

An acre of wheat can produce more than 1500 loaves of bread.

December on this farm is when extra feed needs to be taken out to the cows that are eating in the field. This is where the alfalfa and silage gets mixed together to create a great recipe of feed for cattle.

Just like people need a balanced diet, cows do too. On this farm the cows get a feed ration that has all the food groups cows need.

Thanks for spending a year on the farm with us.

CPSIA information can be obtained
at www.ICGtesting.com
Printed in the USA
BVRC101355021221
622774BV00018B/450